anythink

D0803263

20 FUN FACTS ABOUT AUTO RACING

By Ryan Nagelhout

Gareth Stevens
PUBLISHING

Please visit our website, www.garethstevens.com. For a free color catalog of all our high-quality books, call toll free 1-800-542-2595 or fax 1-877-542-2596.

Cataloging-in-Publication Data

Nagelhout, Ryan.
20 fun facts about auto racing / by Ryan Nagelhout.
p. cm. — (Fun fact file: sports!)
Includes index.
ISBN 978-1-4824-3963-2 (pbk.)
ISBN 978-1-4824-3964-9 (6-pack)
ISBN 978-1-4824-3971-7 (library binding)
1. Automobile racing — Juvenile literature. I. Nagelhout, Ryan. II. Title.
GV1029.13 N34 2016
796.72—d23

First Edition

Published in 2016 by
Gareth Stevens Publishing
111 East 14th Street, Suite 349
New York, NY 10003

Copyright © 2016 Gareth Stevens Publishing

Designer: Sarah Liddell
Editor: Ryan Nagelhout

Photo credits: Cover, pp. 1, 5 Daniel Huerlimann-BEELDE/Shutterstock.com; p. 6 KK Art and Photography/Shutterstock.com; p. 7 Heritage Images/Contributor/Hulton Archive/Getty Images; pp. 8, 10, 11 (background), 29 Action Sports Photography/Shutterstock.com; p. 9 Bryan Busovicki/Shutterstock.com; p. 11 (green and yellow) Ms2ger/Wikimedia Commons; p. 11 (red and checkered) Andrew J. Kurbiko/Wikimedia Commons; p. 11 (black with white stripe and blue with yellow stripe) Denelson 83/Wikimedia Commons; p. 12 Morio/Wikimedia Commons; pp. 13, 20, 24 RacingOne/Contributor/ISC Archives/Getty Images; p. 14 Brian A. Westerholt/Contributor/NASCAR/Getty Images; p. 15 STBR/Wikimedia Commons; p. 16 Robert Alexander/Contributor/Archive Photos/Getty Images; p. 17 Royalbroil/Wikimedia Commons; p. 18 Todd Warshaw/Stringer/Getty Images Sport/Getty Images; p. 19 HodagMedia/Shutterstock.com; p. 21 Nick Laham/Staff/Getty Images Sport/Getty Images; p. 22 Derek Yegan/Shutterstock.com; p. 23 Andy Cross/Contributor/Denver Post/Getty Images; p. 25 AMA/Shutterstock.com; p. 26 Topical Press Agency/Stringer/Hulton Archive/Getty Images; p. 27 (map) Stephen Marques/Shutterstock.com; p. 27 (background) Hulton Archive/Stringer/Hulton Archive/Getty Images.

Printed in the United States of America

CPSIA compliance information: Batch #CW16GS: For further information contact Gareth Stevens, New York, New York at 1-800-542-2595.

Contents

Words in the glossary appear in **bold** type the first time they are used in the text.

The Race Is On

Auto racing is a sport where people make automobiles to race them against each other at different racetracks. There are many different types of auto racing.

The biggest auto racing **circuits** in the world are organized by the kind of car being raced. The National Association for Stock Car Auto Racing, or NASCAR, is the biggest **spectator** sport in the United States. Formula One racing and IndyCar racing use special open-wheeled cars that are superfast. Let's learn more about auto racing!

IndyCar, NASCAR, and Formula One are some of the largest auto racing circuits, but small local races are held on different kinds of racetracks with a number of different automobiles.

Start Your Engines

Engine power in cars is measured using horses!

Horsepower was first used by Scottish inventor James Watt in the 18th century. Watt measured 1 horsepower as the power needed to lift 33,000 pounds (14,968.5 kg) 1 foot (0.3 m) off the ground in 1 minute.

For his measurements, Watt used dray horses, which are about 50 percent stronger than the average horse. This makes horsepower an even odder unit of measurement.

The first auto race was won going 15 miles (24 km) per hour!

The race was held in France in 1895. It ran 732 miles (1,178 km) through France, from Paris to Bordeaux and back to the French capital city. Driver Émile Levassor averaged about 15 miles (24 km) per hour in his Panhard et Levassor car, finishing in just under 49 hours.

Émile Levassor in his Panhard et Levassor car

Later in 1895, the *Chicago Times-Herald* newspaper held the first auto race in America.

FACT 3

There are many different kinds of racetracks.

The simplest track is an oval, which has four left turns. A triangle-shaped speedway has three left turns, while a tri-oval has an extra hump, which gives it five left turns. Road and street courses have many turns, with some going left while others go right!

Talladega Superspeedway is a 2.66-mile (4.28 km) tri-oval where many different series race each year.

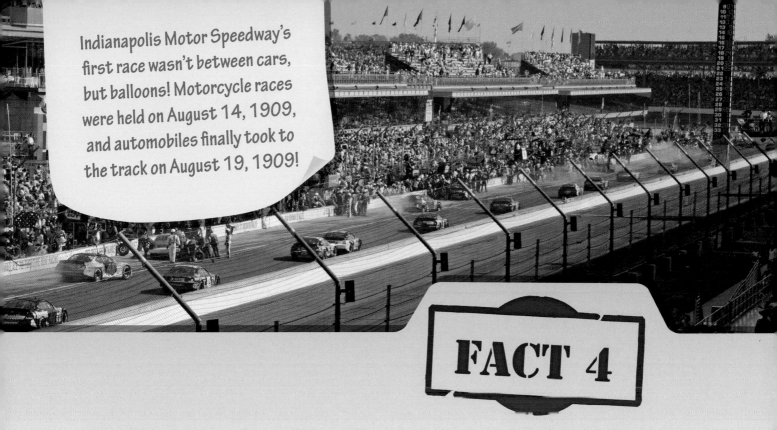

Indianapolis Motor Speedway's first race wasn't between cars, but balloons! Motorcycle races were held on August 14, 1909, and automobiles finally took to the track on August 19, 1909!

FACT 4

Indianapolis, Indiana, is home to the largest racetrack in the world.

Indianapolis Motor Speedway holds more than 250,000 people. The track first opened on June 5, 1909. In 1911, the Indianapolis 500 was held there for the first time. Every year, the Indy 500 is the most popular open-wheeled car race in the United States.

Flagging the Field

Race officials use flags to tell drivers many different things.

A flag waver sits high above the **start/finish line** and lets drivers know what's happening in the race. Drivers also have a radio in their car so their **spotter** can tell them things that are happening on the track.

A driver's crew even uses the radio to tell them how to pass or avoid cars and things they can't see!

10

The Flags of NASCAR

GREEN FLAG
start of race
and restarts

YELLOW FLAG
caution flag, slows cars
down to pace-lap speed

RED FLAG
stops the race

WHITE FLAG
last lap of a race

CHECKERED FLAG
race is over

BLACK FLAG
driver is given a penalty

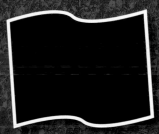

**BLACK FLAG
WITH WHITE STRIPE**
car suspended for not
acting on black flag

**BLUE FLAG WITH
YELLOW STRIPE**
tells cars not on lead lap
to let fast cars go by

FACT 6

The pace car helps drivers get a rolling start in some races.

A pace car, also called a safety car, is used in NASCAR and most IndyCar races to slow cars down on cautions. It also lets them do a "rolling start," which has cars moving across the start/finish line at a certain speed to start a race.

Formula One races do not usually use rolling starts. Instead, cars start the race spread out on the track, not moving, but with their engines on.

Early stock cars had their doors **strapped** or bolted shut. Drivers even used the seat belts that came with the car!

FACT 7

At first, stock car drivers were racing regular cars!

When NASCAR first started, race cars were exactly like cars made in factories. "Stock" meant they couldn't be modified, or changed, in any way. Today, stock cars are named after everyday cars, but they're really specially built race cars.

FACT 8

Richard Petty has nearly twice as many wins as any other driver in NASCAR history!

Nicknamed "The King," Petty won 200 NASCAR races in his **career** before he **retired** in 1992. Second on the list is David Pearson, who has 105 career wins. No other drivers have more than 100 career wins!

Petty also won the Daytona 500 and the NASCAR Championship seven times each in his career.

Bill Elliott drove the fastest car in NASCAR history.

On April 30, 1987, Elliott drove his Ford Thunderbird 212.809 miles (342.483 km) per hour in a **qualifying** lap at Talladega Superspeedway in Alabama. Elliott also holds the track record at Daytona International Speedway—210.364 miles (338.548 km) per hour—which he also set in 1987.

A bad crash at Talladega a few days after Elliot's qualifying run made NASCAR slow down its cars the next season.

FACT 10

NASCAR now actually makes cars go slower at its biggest tracks.

In 1988, NASCAR added a restrictor plate to its cars at Talladega and Daytona. A restrictor plate restricts, or holds back, the engine's power, which forces cars to go slower. NASCAR officials worried about drivers going too fast and causing high-speed **accidents** at its superspeedways.

Restrictor plates make races safer and also more **competitive** because engine speeds are more even between cars.

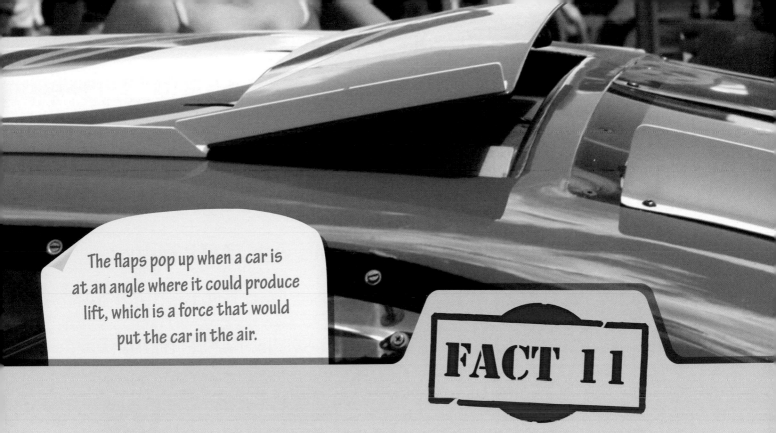

The flaps pop up when a car is at an angle where it could produce lift, which is a force that would put the car in the air.

Flaps of metal keep most NASCAR vehicles from flipping over!

When a car starts spinning out of control in an accident, flaps hidden on the hood and roof of the stock car pop up.

These flaps get in the way of air flowing over the car, pulling the car back to the ground and keeping it from flipping over.

FACT 12

Racing is SAFER, but still dangerous.

Many tracks pad their concrete walls with SAFER barriers, which are softer walls made of steel tubes and hard foam that lessen the force cars have when they hit walls. SAFER barriers were first put in place at Indianapolis Motor Speedway in 2002, and many more tracks now use them.

"SAFER" stands for "Steel and Foam Energy Reduction."

The speed boost now lasts 15 or 20 seconds, depending on the track where the cars are racing.

FACT 13

IndyCar drivers push a button when they want to pass cars.

Since 2012, IndyCars have a push-to-pass button that gives drivers a brief boost of power from their engine. The boost makes it easier to pass cars at high speeds. Today, IndyCar drivers can use the push-to-pass button 10 times during a race.

FACT 14

Sara Christian was the first female driver in NASCAR history.

Christian participated in seven races, finishing in the top 10 twice. Sara's husband, Frank, was the owner of her No. 7/11 Ford. In 1949, Sara and Frank raced against each other at Daytona Speedway!

Sara Christian

Frank finished eighth in the 1949 race, while Sara finished 18th.

Patrick's qualifying time at Daytona was the fastest since 1990. She finished eighth in the race.

FACT 15

Danica Patrick is the only woman to ever win an IndyCar race.

Patrick's win in the 2008 Indy Japan 300 isn't her only groundbreaking accomplishment. She's also the first woman to win a NASCAR Sprint Cup Series **pole**, taking the top qualifying spot at the 2013 Daytona 500.

FACT 16

Races run by the National Hot Rod Association (NHRA) are over in seconds!

Two cars line up side by side and wait for the green light to go! There are lots of different car classes in drag racing, but two of the most popular are 25-foot (7.6 m) Top Fuel cars and Funny Cars.

NHRA races are run on a special, straight track called a drag strip.

No one knows for sure why they're called Funny Cars, but they sure do look strange!

FACT 17

One **cylinder** in a Funny Car engine makes more power than an entire NASCAR engine.

Each cylinder in the 8-cylinder Funny Car engine produces about 750 horsepower. Funny Cars and Top Fuel racers use a gas called nitromethane in their engines to give them even more power—around 7,000 horsepower! That's about 37 times more power than the average street car.

FACT 18

John Andretti

John Andretti was the first driver to pull "Double Duty."

The Indianapolis 500 and a 600-mile NASCAR race in Charlotte, North Carolina, happen on the same day. In 1994, Andretti drove in both! He finished 10th at Indy, then hopped on a plane to Charlotte for the NASCAR race. He had engine trouble and finished 36th.

In 2001, Tony Stewart finished all 1,100 miles (1,770 km) of both races, finishing sixth at Indy and third at Charlotte.

Drivers and teams often test new technology in this tough test of racing skill and endurance.

Le Mans, France, hosts a race that lasts an entire day.

The race, 24 Hours of Le Mans, started in 1923 as a way to test the **endurance** of cars and their drivers. Today, drivers race more than 2,796 miles (4,500 km) straight in the same car!

The Great Race

FACT 20

Drivers raced from New York to Paris in 1908!

Six cars from four countries—the United States, Germany, Italy, and France—left snowy Times Square on February 12, 1908. Drivers went west across the country, then through Japan, Russia, and into Europe. The American car won, making it more than 21,000 miles (33,796 km) to Paris on July 30.

Two newspapers—the *New York Times* in the US and *Le Matin* in France—sponsored the famous race.

winning American Thomas Flyer car

New York to Paris in 1908

PARIS · MOSCOW · OMSK · IRKUTSK · VLADIVOSTOK · YOKOHAMA · VALDEZ · SEATTLE · SAN FRANCISCO · CHICAGO · NEW YORK START FEBRUARY 12

BY CAR —— BY BOAT ---

The winning car—the American Thomas Flyer car driven by George Schuster—had to turn back at Valdez because of bad weather.

The Open Road

There's so much more to auto racing than just going around a track in circles. Racing teams work together to adjust their car to changing track temperatures and what other drivers are doing on the track. There are many different circuits to race, each with different rules about what kind of cars can be used.

The best way to learn more fun facts about auto racing is to get to a track and talk to fans. One trip to the pits, where racers work on their cars, is all you need to fall in love with this fun, superfast sport.

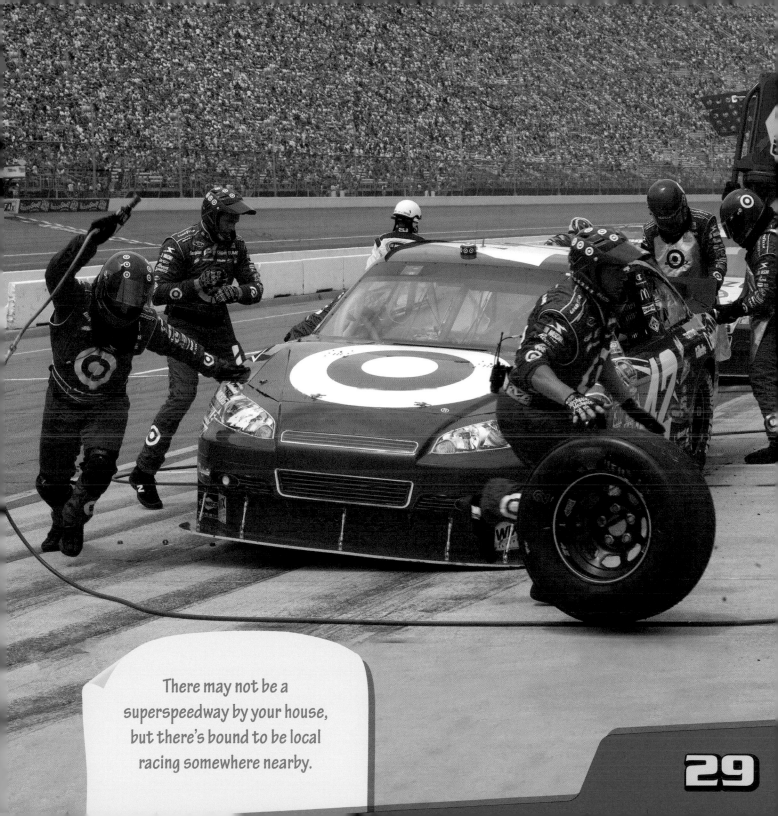

There may not be a
superspeedway by your house,
but there's bound to be local
racing somewhere nearby.

Glossary

accident: a sudden event resulting in loss or injury

career: the job someone chooses to do for a long time

caution: a period of a race where drivers are slowed down due to danger on the track

circuit: a chain of racetracks all running the same type of events . Also, the entire slate of races of one type for a full season.

competitive: able to be won by many different drivers

cylinder: a tube-shaped space in a gasoline engine in which a piston moves up and down to create power

endurance: the ability to last a long time under pressure

pole: the first position in a race

qualify: to be fit to run in a race

retire: to stop racing

spectator: someone watching an event

spotter: a racing team member who tells drivers what's happening on the track

start/finish line: the line where a race begins and each lap is counted

strap: to tie down using a flat piece of material, usually leather

For More Information

Books

Gregory, Josh. *Race Cars: Science, Technology, Engineering.* New York, NY: Children's Press, 2015.

Hantula, Richard. *Science at Work in Auto Racing.* New York, NY: Marshall Cavendish Benchmark, 2012.

Young, Jeff. *Dropping the Flag: Auto Racing.* Edina, MN: ABDO Publishing, 2011.

Websites

IndyCar.com
indycar.com/
Discover more facts about the IndyCar series at the circuit's official website.

National Association for Stock Car Auto Racing
NASCAR.com
The official site of NASCAR has lots of great information about its series and drivers.

What Is NHRA?
nhra.net/streetlegal/whatisNHRA.html
Find more fun facts and learn more about the history of the NHRA here.

Index